Purple Rain: The Stories of My Tears

Written By: Johnathan Jones

Acknowledgements

I want to acknowledge my Lord and savior, Jesus Christ, for comforting me and helping me survive everything that I have endured. "I will never give you too much to bear" is what you said and for that I tell you thank you.

I want to acknowledge my haters, judgers, and attackers. Without you, I wouldn't have the strength, I do have, to keep fighting and to ignore meaningless attacks.

I want to acknowledge my friends and family who have accepted me for who I am and loved me from the beginning. Thank you for standing by myside and encouraging me to keep going.

Dedications

Lastly, I wanted to dedicate this book to my mentors that have continued to shine a light in my life and continued to teach me invaluable lessons.

Sean Strachan	*Mr. Gamble*
Amber Leakway	*Fran. Tucker*
Greg Harrell	*Alvin Lindsey*
Emily Carson	
Latoya and Shelton Cook	

Table Of Contents

Acknowledgements	2
Dedications	2
A Child's Prayer	5
As a… As a	6
Disabled Truth	7
Eat Eat Eat	9
He Made Me This Way	13
I Am An Addict	14
I Feel	17
I Fight	18
I Will Survive	20
Love	21
Meant To Be	23
Not Me But You	25
Pretend	27
Sacrifice	28
Love Me Again	30
This Is Me	32
Time and Time Again	34
Tweet Tweet	37
Hopeless	39
We Are Twins	40
Where is the Sun?	42
You're a Threat	44

Friendless	47
Myself	49
Why Did You?	51
Grand-Daddy	54
On This Day	56
For Every Person	58
Serenity	61
Chance for Love	63
Attention	65
Oh Hattie May	67
Silent No More	69
New Self	71
Resources	73
Author's Bio	74

A Child's Prayer

Inspiration: This poem is the earliest documented poem that I wrote. I was cleaning out my google drive and found this poem I wrote. When I read it for the first time in years, it reminded me of everything I felt when I was a freshman in high school. I believe this poem was my version of a childhood prayer my mom taught me when I was young. This poem is not only a coping mechanism for a 13-year-old boy, but a boy who was pleading to God for help.

Now I sit me down to lunch

To voice my hopes,

I have a bunch.

Give me this day

A sandwich with the crusts cut off of the bread.

(Although I'd rather have a pizza instead.)

Please, help me to make new friends.

Can you make it so recess never ends?

Wish I had toys I saw on TV

And that everyone would like me.

As I sit and close my eyes,

Help those watching me be wise

Please help grown-ups understand

Not every child follows their plan.

As a... As a

Inspiration: This poem was created when I was going through a rough time in life. In this moment, I was feeling depressed and emotionally frustrated. I was trying to come to terms with my sexuality and I felt I had to pretend to be someone else so that I can be accepted and loved by friends and family. With suppressing my personality and other traumatic events in my life, it made me feel that I was never going to find love and that I could never be loved for being true to myself.

As invisible as a ghost

As lonely as a stray

Can someone tell me to stay?

As angry as fire ants

As sad as dark clouds

Why can't love be allowed

As tired as a machine

As drained as a pipe

For some reason I keep saying it's life

As confused as a kid

As disappointed as a society

Why has this become my reality

As I lay wondering about alibis

I continued to be paralyzed

No matter the emotion

I don't make my problems a big commotion

Push, Digress, and Smile

Because nobody really cares for miles

Risk being yourself

And it's back to feeling as small as an elf

Disabled Truth

Inspiration: This poem was created based on my perspective of living as a disabled person. Since the age of 6, I was diagnosed with Leg Calve Perthes Disease, and since then it has progressed significantly over time. Currently, I am dependent on a walker to assist me with moving from place to place. Living with this disability and being the only person with a physically disability in school, church, and even my family, has made me feel alone and out of place. Over time, I started feeling like I didn't deserve to take up space because I was "crippled". My former high school even lightly punished (1-Day In-School Suspension) a white male student who sent me a death threat via school email. All my life I felt that I would never be any good to anyone because I was seen as damaged.

Excuse me

Can I

May you

Please

Words I say everyday

Maybe the awkwardness will fade a way

Eww

Disappointing

Broken

Damaged

Things I hear that brings me to tears

Hoping love will find a way

Stares

Discrimination

Judgement

Rudeness

The things I experience on the daily

Without one moment of peace

Loneliness

Shameful

Trashy

Hindrance

Thoughts that try to cloud my mind

Trying to remember the good times

After a while, an understanding grows

That good means okay

Accessible means outdoor ramp

Help means underfunded systems

Will things ever be good

Can things truly be accessible

Time will tell

Some people try

And organizations fail

As they turn a blind eye

Eat Eat Eat

Inspiration: This poem was created during one of my weight-loss attempts. Since birth, I was always a heavy-set kid. When I was born, I weighed 10 pounds and my weight just continued to grow throughout my life. All my life, my family couldn't understand why I was eating so much and why I could never get full. My family always talked to me about healthy eating and trying to lose weight, but as a kid it just felt like they were judging me. At that time, I was eating to comfort myself during my childhood traumas. So anytime I was feeling upset, emotional, or bored, I went to food to help comfort me. My family actually coined the term, "Eat Eat Eat" because during their "You Need To Lose Weight Speech" they would say that I was always eat eat eating. Hearing that constantly and feeling like no one was trying to understand me, it made me turn to food more. It didn't help either that everyone was saying that I need to lose weight but they would always give me foods that they say I shouldn't have. This poem is my emotional release of all my weight and food problems. It has helped me forgive and overcome some of the things that I've endured.

Eat Eat Eat

To handle the pain

Eat Eat Eat

To feel okay

Eat Eat Eat

To control the stress

Eat Eat Eat

Will always be what you do best

Eat Eat Eat

Are words that I know

Words that I hate so

Eat Eat Eat

Is what I was always told

But only if they really knew

Eat Eat Eat

Was my way of getting high

Like disappearing from reality

When life is such a tragedy

Eat Eat Eat

Is what I used to cope

I would eat and drink everything

Eat Eat Eat

Was my language of love

Eat Eat Eat

Was my signal of distress

Eat Eat Eat

Is something that truly made me weak

Instead of enjoying taste

I had to deal with the guilt and the shame

To myself I plea

This is all a mistake

Eat Eat Eat

Is what I do

And it gave me a lot of problems too

Eat Eat Eat

Was great in the moment

I just don't do it for enjoyment

When I Eat Eat Eat

I just keep think think thinking

That today might be the end

My heart might stop beating

Because Eat Eat Eat

Is all I do

Because who else can I run to

Eat Eat Eat

Was my main man

But I need help to see

That Eat Eat Eating

It's not the right path for me

He Made Me This Way

Inspiration: This poem was created to remind me that God made me exactly how I am. Identifying with multiple oppressed minorities, has positive and negative efforts on one's mind (my own opinion). Being a part of multiple minorities, I forget that my value is not minor or minute. I had to learn that my value is not determined by my situation nor the opinions of others. This poem is a reminder that regardless of your sexuality, race, nationality, gender, or any other demographic characteristics you were made exactly you were meant to be.

I feel beautiful in many ways

People can't see it

But they only see what is outside of me

I want a compliment or two

I want some love and free food

But time after time

I'm treated like a dime

Feeling so worthless and small

And only if they can see me for who I am

The pain I endured made me who I am

My undying faith has made me who I am

My family has made me who I am

My victimization has made me who I am

My DNA has made me who I am

I am who I am because I never gave up

I am who I am because I never let go

I am who I am because I have God

And because I have God I will never fail

Because I have God I will never be defeated

Because I have God I knew it was already worked out

My pain is temporary because he made it that way

Though I may be sad right now

Though I may be hurting right now

Though I may be in pain right now

Though I may be stressed right now

I know that

He will make a Way

I Am An Addict

Inspiration: This poem was created as an emotional release. When I wrote this poem, I just started my journey for bariatric surgery and I was using writing as my coping mechanism to avoiding eating. I was thinking of how people don't usually talk about how food can be an addiction. In my personal opinion, I feel that dealing with a food addiction is one of the harder addictions; due to the fact that you have to eat to survive and you will be constantly surrounded around your triggers. After accepting that food is an addiction for me, I looked up the known 12-step method for recovery that various addiction support groups use. One of those steps is to acknowledge you have a problem and that your will isn't strong enough to overcome it alone. This poem is a physical representation of me acknowledging my addiction and my hope for a better and healthier future.

The smell that it blows

The comfort it gives me

The love it makes me feel

The emotions it solves

It had my trust

But I have to say enough is enough

I am an addict

Controlled by something I eat daily

I am an addict

Influenced by a voice and a feeling

I am an addict

Restricted to only saying yes and to indulge

I am an addict

My love for the taste conquers all

My life

Was food

My life

Survived on food

My life

Needs food

To have a desire to stop

But bonded by life's needs

It's like rats in a cage

The rats wants to be free

And its efforts only kills them in the end

I am an addict

Dragged through the consequences of yesterday

And judged for my uncontrolled actions

I am an addict

An addict who cries and pleads

Wondering why foods means so much to me

I am an addict

To acknowledge my disease and label

Is step one of saying

That I am able

I am able to overcome

I am able to survive

I am able to live

My addiction is my history

Not my future

I Feel

Inspiration: This poem was created when I started to see a therapist to help surpass the traumas that I have endured and to allow me to be more connected to my feelings. During one of our conversations, she asked me what are my coping mechanisms, except for food, I told her writing, singing, and cooking. Acknowledging my writing as a coping mechanism, she wanted me to start writing poems when I felt triggered to eat. Later that week, I had some frustration with the lack of support for the disability community in Georgia and I wanted to write a poem to describe how I was feeling. Once I started, I started generalizing the poem to fit all my feelings that I felt that week. This poem was one of my first poems that I wrote. (With some recent edits)

I feel the heat from their eyes

The judgment from their stares

Like a mosquito in a house

I feel out of place

I feel embarrassed

Like I should be ashamed

My own family has some part to blame

I feel awkward and weird

Lord help me through this and be my shield

Can't wait for that day

The day my weight will go away

Lord remind me that you are with me

To comfort me in how I feel

I Fight

Inspiration: This poem was created as a call-to-action. When writing this poem, I wanted to express my will to continue fighting every obstacle that comes my way. I felt that writing this will give me more courage, strength, and hope. Knowing that I continued fighting regardless of how it looked, is not only inspirational but admirable. This poem speaks to anyone who is oppressed or going through a rough time. The message in this poem is to keep fighting and that failure is just a direction to lead you to success.

Like a Butterfly in a net

I fight

Like a Chicken being lined up for slaughter

I fight

As someone living in poverty

Being judged by society

I fight

Fighting for a chance for love

Fighting for a chance to learn

Fighting for my loved ones

Fighting to continue growing & living

I will continue to fight

Because when I stop fighting

I have truly lost sight

Sight of my dreams

Sight of my goals

Sight of my supporters

And Sight of my purpose

My Advice

Continue to fight and stand

For your journey has just began

I Will Survive

Inspiration: This poem was influenced after my public coming out on social media. Even though I received loved from many people. I still didn't receive the acceptance and love from some of the people that mean so much to me. After coming out publicly, it caused some difficult and tense conversation. Handling those conversations and the aftermath of coming out was challenging and it made me feel that I was on the verge of giving up on hope. Then, in a moment, I realized that my entire life has been about trying to please others, and at some point, I have to live my life for me and no one else. This poem is my song of endurance and bravery. It symbolizes that even though my feelings may be hurt and things may never change, that I will survive through it all, because God's love is all I need.

Like a season

I change

Like water

I ripple

Like skin

I bruise

These things remind me that

My pain is real and true

That every cut

Feels like a knife in the gut

That every tear

Reminds me of my mother's fears

That every headache

Reminds me that everyone makes mistakes

My pain has created a story

A story that tries to stick to me like lies

Lies that I won't abide

I may be marked up

I may not be the right fit for clubs

But like God's Love

I will survive

Love

Inspiration: This poem was my jealously peeking through my emotions. I was feeling alone, because it felt that everyone my age has at least been in love once, and I have never been in love or loved by anyone. With the lack of affection from guys, I was upset at myself for being what I thought was "unattractive". It took me some time to understand that I am beautiful and that any man who cannot see that is not the person who I want to be with. However, it still sucked that I never had a real boyfriend to talk about with friends and family. This poem, honestly, was me being jealous of what some of my friends had; which was love. Nowadays, this poem just serves as memories of how I felt and how important affection is, even for single people.

I seem them all

They are cute

Handsome, Cool

And blissfully thin

Oh, how I dream

Of an alternative reality

Where I date, love, and grow

I feel that love is an object that I have been rejected to have

To have love is to have enjoyment

To have love is to never be alone

To have love is to be understood

To have love is to be blessed

Because everyone is not blessed enough to ever feel love

So, stop complaining

Stop hating

Stop wasting time

And enjoy your gift

The gift of love

Meant To Be

Inspiration: This is actually a song that I wrote and not a poem. I wrote this song because being rejected (in some aspects) and judged by others, it made me question is this what God has for me. I wasn't necessarily questioning God; I was questioning the events that have happened in my life. In this moment, I was thinking about all the judgement, hatred, and bigotry that I've experienced. So, I had to just sing how I was feeling and this song just come out. As a social worker, it definitely speaks to what I want to do with my career and how I want to advocate for others' rights.

In one moment

I can feel hopeless

Because of what they say

In one action

Makes me react and

I just need a break

Is this whom I meant to be

To be judged by them

To be viewed as less than

Is this my prophecy

To be struggling with life

To always fighting

In one dream it

No one cares if

I'm big, able, or gay

In my reality

There's some cruelty

Because of societies ways

Is this whom I meant to be

To be judged by them

To be viewed as less than

Is this my prophecy

To be struggling with life

To always fighting

I can't walk by

And not just fight

Fight for all my rights

I can't behave

Because I'm afraid

Gotta stand up and say, hey

Is this whom I meant to be

To be judged by them

To be viewed as less than

Is this my prophecy

To be struggling with life

To always fighting

Is this whom I meant to be

To be judged by them

To be viewed as less than

Is this my prophecy

To be struggling with life

To always fighting

Not Me But You

Inspiration: This poem was created during a time where I started to refuse to be labeled as the offender for being black, gay, and disabled. This was my version of saying enough is enough to all the people who judged me and made me feel less than. I wrote this poem because I've withheld my feelings for so long and I needed to release them and to stand up to my attackers/offenders. This poem is me calling them out and saying that they can no longer label me nor convince me that I am a problem; I also mention in the poem that they have to answer to God for what they've done.

After all this time

I'm finding out it's not me

I'm not the problem

I'm not the cause of my pain

I'm not the offender

But merely the victim of a broken system

They wanted me to feel broken

They wanted me to feel misplaced

They wanted me to feel damaged

So that I could never sore and be determined

I'm no longer lost

I'm no longer depressed

Because God helped me realize

That I was wonderfully made

With the help of a friend or two

I was able to say "I'm threw"

I'm threw with accepting ableism crap

I'm threw with telling myself I have a problem

I'm threw being a punching bag

Because I'm worth more

I desire more

And I demand more

The truth is

Not me but you

Have a problem

Not me but you

Need help

Not me but you

Need to reevaluate your actions

Because if you don't

Not me but you

Will have God to answer to

Pretend

Inspiration: This poem was created while I've been attempting to overcome my trust issues. With this poem, I was able to express a constant state of questioning and personality suppression. I named this poem pretend, because I had to pretend a lot of my feelings in life. The message in this poem is to be yourself and be honest with yourself and others.

Mouths talking

Words hurting

You're not helping

Hand holding

Friends caring

Can I be this trusting

Back stabbing

Shit speaking

Only if I knew what I was seeking

Continued questioning

Getting frustrating

Just pretend to be smiling

Time is winding

Never hearing

My truth is blinding

Sacrifice

Inspiration: I created this poem because I wanted to express my pain along with the sacrifice that I have gave. With my disability, I had to give up on many things that I wanted to do because my disability limited me. I was unable to achieve all the things that I wanted to do. This poem illustrates the emotions between sacrificing and the lack of accomplishment. I wanted to show that it's okay to feel that you are losing everything you desire, because when you hit rock bottom is when you see the world with a new perspective, and that is where you will find your true purpose.

I don't want to

But I have no choice

Who else is going to help me

I'm not about to go begging please

As a man I have to do

What I gotta do

My heart is in pain

How many times am I expected

To lose everything just to win

I'm trying to catch up

But it's extremely tough

No one has made me an offer

A helping hand or two

I'm tired of being the family member with no money too

Working like a dog just to survive

God please send me a sign

My future is unclear

My freedom is unclear

My health is unclear

God please don't let my work be in vain

I've sacrificed too much

I've missed so many things

This has to mean something

Or is this just a sick game

Lord I pray

That all my problems go away

That I may reap all the seeds I have sowed

One step at a time

It's going to be alright

I'm sure Jesus will be by my side

Love Me Again

Inspiration: This is a poem I created when I was frustrated with some of my family members. When I came out to them as gay, they said they loved me but that I was living in an abomination of a lifestyle. When hearing that from the people you consider to be "loved ones", it felt that they stop loving me as a person. So, I wanted to ask them to love me again as a person, as a family member, and as a brother in Christ. This poem is everything I wanted to say to my family back then but never had the courage to tell them.

I sit here and cry

Thinking of why?

You tell me you love me

Then act so ugly

I tried so hard to please

So what you feel can ease

But all you do is dictate

And spread your nasty hate

I can't do it anymore

It's just not what I adore

You say it's wrong to be with men

And that you love me but not the sin

But every time you speak

My heart keeps getting weak

You cast me down

Where I just drown

Even though I try so hard

I still remind scarred

It has to stop

I can't keep putting you on top

I have to live my life

Cause if I don't I might use a knife

You may never treat me the same

And point at the devil for the blame

But it's you who makes me feel

So unworthy, I don't think I can heal

I just wished you'd understand

That I want you to Love Me Again

This Is Me

Inspiration: I created this poem because I wanted people to stop seeing me as the "poor disabled guy". I wanted people to see my personality and not to judge me based on my circumstances and looks. When I wrote this, I wanted to show people that I'm more than their words and that I will still continue to grow with or without their love.

When you see me

Do you really see the real me?

You might see me as disabled

But when I look in the mirror

I say I am able

You might call me dark skinned

But I tell myself I have beauty within

You tease me for being feminine

For God has created this fine specimen

You try to bound me with your words

But I have dealt with worse

You sling your belt of judgement

However, you lack basic fundaments

That God is love

And he wants us to rise above

So just know that your hate

Won't instigate

Because I am my ancestor's dream

They fought for me to be free

And proudly I say, This Is Me!

Time and Time Again

Inspiration: This poem was my efforts to advocate for black and brown individuals. This poem expresses the frustration, rage, and disappointment that black and brown individuals feel all around America. I called this poem Time and Time Again because police brutality, systemic racism, racial hate crimes, and discrimination still remain at high volumes in America. I wrote this poem to wake people up and ask, "Are you listening? Are you seeing the damage that is being done? If so, what are you doing to help?". In the beginning stages of writing, I started by trying to "sugar-coat" the truth, but then I realized that if this poem can make someone uncomfortable then I've accomplished my goal; which is to explain in detail the damage that the black/brown community endures. A friend, an ally, a leader, a pastor, and anyone in a caring role or relationship will answer the call to action to help end systemic racism in the United States.

Time and time again

I don't know where to begin

All lives matter they say

But only for the rich and white, Hooray

They want to remind us

That there is no justice

For we are technically free

But are we truly

Squished on the ground like a sponge

Asking Lord what have I done

Screaming for momma and praying for ease

Only to be left saying I can't breathe

Time and time again

The system has failed

Only for us to try and prevail

We try to sleep peacefully at night

But the lord only knows what demons come to fright

You were sleeping and unarmed

But they say it was a false alarm

A mistake that cost a queen her life

But they don't care because she wasn't white

Time and time again

We protest and rally

While cops try to wreak havoc and tally

We have the right to be free

But what am I supposed to believe

I just can't be me

When I have to worry about my safety

Can't wear a hoodie and exercise

For they will shoot their guns and end our lives

What can I do

Cause time and time again

We try

We fight

And we lose

For they want us to believe we are free

But those are lies you see

Systemic racism

Racial poverty

Low-income neighborhoods

And what they call the hood

We are pawns in their game

Repeating every move

But bond to a continuous cycle

Time and time again

I wanted to give up on hope

But Harriet Tubman wouldn't let me

Martin Luther King Jr wouldn't let me

Emmett Till wouldn't let me

Brianna Taylor wouldn't let me

And Trayvon Martin wouldn't let me

The answer is simple

Fight for the home we want for our kids

Our kids with the innocence of an angel

Our kids who have to learn to be proud of their skin

Our kids who will tell their kids of how we fought for our home

Let's stop the continuous cycle

Let's rally the troops

Let's rally the allies

Raise the flags of battle

And sound the horns of triumph

Victory is upon us

Because time and time again

We have overcome

Tweet Tweet

Inspiration: This poem was my first poem that I ever wrote for an emotional coping tool. I made this poem because I was thinking about how hard I have been trying in life to survive and to overcome many obstacles; while, I was thinking about that I

couldn't help but compare it to a bird. A bird has to continue to fight to live and to not get eaten. It has to continue to fight and learn to fly. It has to continue to fight to find a home and to build a nest somewhere. Birds have to fight a lot and this poem illustrates me as the bird. The only thing with this story is that the bird dies by suicide and gave up on hope. At that time in my life, I didn't have hope and I guess I wanted to create a scenario where someone or something else could feel how I felt. This poem can be interrupted in different ways. You can view this poem as inspirational, because it reminds you that you survived feeling like this, or you can view it as depressing and you don't want to feel as hopeless as the bird.

Tweet Tweet

The birdie goes

Wondering if he will survive

Going day to day

Wondering if the pain will go away

Tweet Tweet

The birdie cries

Feeling it all inside

Because no one really wants to know why

And he feels like he might die

Tweet Tweet

The birdie screams

Hoping it's all a dream

Knowing that he is on the edge

Soon facing defeat

Tweet Tweet

The birdie sighs

Knowing it's time to say goodbye

Having no one by his side

It was time

The bird has died

Tweet tweet

Was a sound that a birdie made

But life was so terrible

The birdie couldn't stand the pain

Hopeless

Inspiration: When I created this poem, I was in a disappointed mood. I felt that my efforts were going in vain. This poem illustrates how annoyed I was with trying and never succeeding. After so many failures, it started to affect my confidence and hope negatively. I started feeling hopeless and insecure. After rereading the poem recently, it makes me want to advocate for mental health professionals in all areas of education.

Why do I try

I end up hurting myself even worse

I accepted this

But others gave me hope

I thought I was free

But again, I have to admit I'm lonely

This feeling sucks

My heart hurts

And I feel stupid for having hope

Like who am I

I'm the guy that has never loved

The guy who has never been loved

I'm the guy that was given pity love

And the guy who was never put first

When will I learn

To stop trying

We Are Twins

Inspiration: I wrote this poem about me and my best friend of 5+ years. We have been through many things together over the years. We went to the same undergraduate university (Fort Valley State University), and when we were getting ready to graduate, we had to decide which university we wanted to go to. We both agreed that we were going to make our graduate decisions without thinking of the other person. This, amongst other things, caused some tension between us. This was one of the longest arguments/disagreements we have ever had. I created this poem because I didn't want to lose my friend. This poem's meaning is that if the relationship means anything then try to resolve the situation, because time is continuous. Once you have spent that much time with someone, make the effort to fix the problem so your time is not wasted.

See, I'm sitting up here

Worrying about my feelings

Trying to make it

Even when I can't change it

There is so much I wanna do

I'm just trying to make it through

Feeling like there is no hope

And nothing to hold onto

I'm trying to fight everyday

Wishing the pain just goes away

The honest truth

Is that I think about you

Worrying that this maybe it

But honestly that's bullshit

Through all the pain

We have endured

I refuse to let this be

The way it all ends

We are twins not by blood

But by love we have won

So, no more fights can make damage

Because we have Jesus

And his love can heal unlike any bandage

Where is the Sun?

Inspiration: This poem is a metaphor for life. In this poem, the sun represents light and goodness, and the sun is currently missing and can't be found. This metaphor is relevant because sometimes we have a lot of bad things happen to us and it becomes harder and harder to see the sun and to keep fighting to survive. This poem illustrates the common questions and circumstances that people say and feel when dealing with a lot on their shoulders. I feel that this poem can help someone understand that, even when the bad things come and you are wondering where is the light during the crisis, that as long as you keep looking you will find the light one day.

Storms thundering

Rain Pouring

Where is the Sun?

Earth Quaking

Lives Shaken

Is this just a sick pun?

Winds are blowing

Cars are crashing

This isn't fun

One argument

Leads to one's pain

Two adults

Leads to miscommunication

Three chances

Leads to three disappointments

Where is the sun?

Standing in Darkness

Wondering why me?

Where is the Sun?

You're a Threat

Inspirations: This is my most recent poem that I have written and performed. This poem started as a thought. I was at work thinking about my skin color, and how people hated me because of it. It had me thinking of the reasons of why police officers or any other white superracist would want to kill and to harm black/brown individuals. Once I started to think of the reasons, I couldn't stop brain storming writing materials for my thoughts. So, I started typing and the words started to flow from my heart to my brain and onto a virtual document. This poem is definitely one of my best works. This poem illustrates what the black/brown community loves about their complexion and their culture, and this poem also illustrates the minds of racist police officers aiming to kill and harm colored people. This poem is taking place as if a black/brown person was pulled over and is now being asked to come out of the car to be arrested. My goal for this poem was to graphicly explain the contents of arresting a black/brown person. I wanted to show that to some officers, being black/brown is already a crime. I wanted to show that when the officers come in with a preconceive notion about somebody and they allow their emotions, like fear, to control their action; that's when people that look like me, die with excessive force. This poem is in honor of all the black/brown lives that are killed daily by the system. This poem is for the black/brown community, and to advocate for our rights. This poem is speaking towards Caucasian people, Hispanic people, Gay people, and any other person, it's time to end this genocide of colored people. This poem is a call-to-action. My question is who will answer the call?

The darkness of my skin

The glistening of my brown tone

STOP

Hands behind your head

My unique culture

My creative swag

STOP

Move your hands slowly

The melanin in my skin

And the will to live

STOP

You are not allowed to talk

It's me projecting my voice

And my will to fight

STOP

Stop resisting arrest

It's my beating heart

And my beautiful breath

STOP

Stop Trying to live

Your race makes you a threat

Your blackness makes you a treat

Your comb makes you dangerous

Your sleep is our opportunity

Your breathe is ours to take

Your life belongs to us

You are just collateral damage

Like pot holes in the street

The damages are inevitable

And they don't matter

Because All Lives Matter

I shouldn't give

For others to benefit

You can grow just like me

But only if you weren't a threat

Friendless

Inspiration: I created this poem when I felt invisible from society. At that time, I felt that I have tried so many ways to make friends and nothing was working. I felt that maybe the problem was my personality or who I was as a person. My self-esteem was just being attacked by my anxiety, and I couldn't stop thinking of "semi-truths". I have friends who communicate with people who dislike me, and I think the fact of my friends being okay with that made me feel like my friends liked me out of pity. With being in so many minorities, it sometimes gets challenging determining who is actually trying to be a friend and who is just showing me pity. This poem is my attempt to reaffirm myself.

The way I feel when I'm around people new

The way people look at me as I enter the room

The way people tend not to like me

I'm trying not to let it affect me

But it's hard when it's unveiling

My friend list is low

My supporters are at a minimum

My self-esteem is spiraling

I can be bold, confident, and spirited

But they keep judging me on my personality

I try to be their friends, their confidants

But they rather keep their distance and hide

I have an amazing spirit

I am a nice person and a caring friend

I am Godly and understanding

But apparently that's not enough

Oh, I don't wanna see

That the problem is me

But what else can I do

When everyone is saying it's you

Alone, afraid, and sad

That's my storyline

Not being able to maintain a social life

They see me and run

And I don't know why

But when will it be my time

To make friends, to laugh, and to shine

Myself

Inspiration: I created this poem as a release of all the negative emotions I have been feeling. When I wrote this poem, I was recently sexually violated by someone who was becoming a friend. I have been violated before, but this time was different. After I was violated, I told people who I considered loved ones. Their response was more shame and judgement. I even got in heated conversations with those loved ones, and still to this day it's a sore topic. Looking back at it, I wished that I never spoke up. Because in that moment, the people who I expected to stand by me, left me behind emotionally. I definitely advocate for sexual violence victims to speak out when they feel safe to do so, and I should have waited until I knew if my heart was safe. This poem is more than my pain, but my tears. The lesson I learned from this is that sometimes you have to fight for yourself, because no one will fight harder for yourself than you.

When the times comes

Can I count on you

When I need you the most

Will you be there for me

When I've been hurt by someone

Will you fight for me.

These things I wonder

What may happen

When everything is on the line

What will happen

When I feel alone and I want to cry

What will happen

When I hide my true feelings inside

I see that yall want me to be different

Yall want me to feel different

Yall want me to act differently

Yall want someone that's not me

When problems come

Do I have to face it myself

When situations arise

Do I have to pray for myself

When I'm feeling down and sad

Do I just hope that loniless is the cure

Alone

The pedagogy of my life

Discriminated

The perspective of my existence

Insecurities

My secret identity

What more can I do then be myself

How else can I act, but myself

Who am I supposed to be except myself

I feel alone, discriminated, and insecure

But I also feel empowered

Empowered to be myself no matter the time

Because it's my life that's on the line

So stop asking me why

Because honey you are out of time

I've fought my battles

I've rosed to the occasion

And without your help

And with God's unwavering will

I made it

Why Did You?

Inspiration: This poem was created as a song when I felt betrayed by a friend. I felt that I was willing to do more than they were for our friendship. At this time, I was upset because I felt that they weren't trying to understand me and that they were shaming me for something that wasn't my fault. This song is one of the most emotional songs I have written, because I wrote this about someone who I care for very much. Thinking about it now, it makes me upset sometimes, but I refuse to let our friendship end because of someone's actions. I know that me and that person are great friends, and that we both share mutual love between each other. However, in this moment, I felt alone and unloved.

Why did you have to leave me

Why do you have to take her side

Why do you have to hurt me

Was all this a lie

I thought we were more than this

You've always had my back

Why did you have to go

I feel

All alone

All alone

I feel

All Alone

All Alone

Why do they pick on me

Why do they always break my heart

But can it be

That it was always me

I thought I was very kind

But I see that was just a line

Cause they want me

To feel

All Alone

All Alone

To feel

All Alone

All Alone

I just can't take anymore

I just want my story of gold

Can't I just be

Freaking happy

Why do they hurt me so bad

 Can I …. Just breath

Without them abusing me

I wanna be free

Why do yall have to say these things

Is there something wrong with me

I just want the pain to end

You all hate me

That's why I'm

All Alone

All Alone

That's why I'm

All Alone

Alone

Grand-Daddy

Inspiration: My granddaddy passed away this past July and it was hard for me to come to terms with the fact he was gone. Earlier that week, I kept saying to myself that I need to call him and just like that he's gone. While planning for the funeral, I wanted to say a few words in honor of everything he has taught me. He was such a loving persona and he loved the Lord so much. When I told him that I was gay he just said okay. My granddaddy was so influential to everyone he met. This poem is in honor of him. Love granddaddy and I will see you one day soon.

A word or two

Can only sum up only a few

My granddaddy was more

More than I ever known

So many memories coming back

Like I'm having an emotional attack

This is hard to accept

I thought I had more time left

Now that he's gone up in the sky

I'm sad inside that I did not say goodbye

He taught me discipline for sure

Like me and JJ were locked outside the door

He cared about us and our future

He taught me to be a trooper

He gave me a chance to use my voice

And God showed up and all rejoiced

We prayed and praise together

I will always remember

He taught me so much in little time

Time I wished was on my side

I'm glad he wasn't in any pain

Because he deserves peace in every way

Love, Kindness, and Family was him

And it won't be the same without 'em

I know he would want us to stay strong

And know that God's work is not done

He was a light in our lived

And he'd always shined bright

On This Day

Inspiration: I wrote this poem as a way to advocate for the multiple lives lost with police brutality and racial discrimination in our nation. This poem references the meaning of Independence Day for people of color. How people of color were not free and how slavery still existed. This poem is not to disrespect the brave women, men, and non-binary people who have served this country. This poem is for them. This poem is for all racial minorities. This poem is for the entire world. That we need to come together and stop racism, police brutality, and blatant discrimination. On this day, lets make a change for the betterment of this nation.

On this day

We celebrate with rejoice

On this day

We honor our history

On this day

We remember why we are free

But in this day and age

Are we really free?

As we continue to fill the skies with color

We have to remember "our history and present culture

That this day wasn't meant for me and you

That this day is a celebration for white freedom and the few

We call it Independence Day

But when can I be free I say

That it seems to always rain on my parade

That I can never stop being afraid

Because the truth is they still see me as a slave

In the eyes of the system we praise

They see people like me and think A

Why do they get to breathe

In a system that was made by white supremacist

You think the government would have fix this

Where black people are discriminated by the law

And where immigrants are being stalled

Where women are told what to do with their bodies

And where disabled people are told their nobodies

Where gay and lesbian people are told there abominable

And where plus size people are viewed as intolerable

Where trans people are being killed in the streets

And where guns are continued to be used to stop our children's heartbeats

This is the reality

Of our society

That this day is for the white men

Not me and my kin

On this day

I refuse to celebrate our tragedy

On this day

I'm standing up societal pressure and saying

On this day,

Let's rise and speak for our neighbors

Because on this day

We are all in this together

On this day

Let's demand what we deserve

Because our freedom should start today

For Every Person

Inspiration: I created this poem when the United States Supreme Court overturned Roe v. Wade. As an effect of the supreme court's decisions, states can enforce any abortion law, including a total ban of the procedure.

To me, this poem was an attempt to advocate for women's rights. As a cisgender male, I can acknowledge that I do not understand the various challenges that women endure; however, I do understand how it feels to be picked on. I wanted to create a poem that spoke on the rights of women but also acknowledge the oppression that has been filtered through multiple minorities. Though this poem may not change the hearts of politicians, I feel it will hopefully let someone know they are not invisible.

It's a sad day in America

A day we all have seen coming

Where female rights have been called into question

And where there is no order

We say we want equality and peace

But yet we tell women what to do with their bodies

We have some societal standards

That would be too much for anyone to handle

While some men shout and bark on what is right

Other men and women continue to fight

Because why do men get to do what they please

But they don't have to submit their bodies

Where men get more pay

And women don't have a say

We think this is the end

But honey it's about to begin

Because they have started a domino effect

That just creates a big ole mess

Today they say women abide by man's will

Tomorrow there will be an anti-gay marriage bill

When they come for one minority

They come for us all

Because we have to stand tall

So that every woman and child

And every colored-skinned and foreign person

And every gay, lesbian, bisexual, transgender, and queer individuals

And any other person who is different can say

WE ARE VISIBLE

AND WE WILL NOT BE IGNORED

Because where there is unity there is equity

And equity can bring equality.

And equality is what this country really needs

This country needs every person to have a voice

To fight against the injustice.

Serenity

Inspiration: For all my life food has been my support system. I was known as an emotional binge eater. Whenever, I felt an emotion I would get the undesirable hunger to eat. This hunger felt like it could never be filled. After I made the choice to undergo weight-loss surgery, I didn't expect some of the mental effects on my mind. After surgery, I my relationship to food wasn't the same. It became a distant stranger that I cordially meet. With my relationship to food being destroyed, I was left without a decent coping mechanism to help me cope and process everything that I was going through. Not having a coping mechanism was something that me and my former therapist did not expect. This poem is a prayer that I wrote because praying has always made me feel comfort, and since I couldn't binge, praying was the only thing left I could do to receive comfort. This poem was my hope for serenity.

My emotions are high

Temptations are on my mind

Trying not to indulge in Food

But how else can I change my mood

Food was my comfort

Life made me feel discomfort

And not indulging in my cravings fully

Makes me feel so naked and silly

I'm just so emotional

And without food I'm vulnerable

Like animals, I feel naturally unclothed

With all of my emotions being showed

Without my comforting shield

I need something that can heal

I know my scars and my reasons

But only Jesus can really see us

He knows my story so well

He written every detail

I know that this is all in his plans

But God I'm just one man

At times I feel so pressured

But God keeps reminding me

There's a lesson

Lord help me with these emotions

So my life can go on

Amen

Chance for Love

Inspiration: Ever since grade school, I suffer from low self-esteem and lack of confidence. I was always the kid who was different then everyone else. I was bigger than everyone else. I wasn't abled like everyone else. "I wasn't normal like everyone else" is what I believe. At one point, I started calling myself fat and ugly, because I thought if I just accepted that then it wouldn't hurt so bad when kids made fun of me. When I started, figuring out my sexuality, I felt that maybe this is the reason why I haven't found love, but even when I came out, it wasn't any better; at times, it felt so much worse. Having a non-accepting family and then having kids who also teased me daily, it made me feel that I was unworthy of love. I felt that I was dealt all the wrong cards when I was born, and love wasn't in my cards. When I was young, I attempted so many times to get attention from any and everybody. I just wanted to feel loved, noticed, and accepted. I wrote this poem when I was talking with a guy who seemed to like me very much. After some time, I found out he didn't like me as much as I thought. However, it was that moment that maybe a guy could love me. I thought maybe there is a chance for me to find love. So I wrote this snippet of a song to maybe encourage myself to have hope that love will come.

I'd had no hope in love

Thought I didn't deserve it

I could've never seen

That He said he loved me

I'd thought I would be alone

But he continued to surprise me

And now I know

There's a chance

A chance for Love

Chance for love

Chance for love

When I came out

I felt like the black sheep of the family

Always in and out

Of conversations about me

And I felt unloved

That I would lose my only family

But then he said those words

And now I know

There's a chance

A chance for love

Chance for love

Chance for love

Attention

Inspiration: As a disabled person, I had to learn that people sometimes don't like to accommodate for you. For me and my disability, it affects my mobility. It's hard for me to walk/stand for long periods of times and walk at a steady pace. Due to my disability, it has made dating and making new friends hard. This poem was inspired because I was experiencing what it feels to be left behind physically. I had some friends who hated to wait for me to catch up or hated that I had to take breaks to sit down. I never understood why. This poem represents me asking them.

I try to get by in life

But why can't you see me

I'm dying inside

I'm waiting for you to notice

That I'm sitting here hopelessly

Feeling so freaking lonely

I just want to be seen

For my personality

I can't stop

But think you don't

See or care for who I have become

You don't even text or call my phone

Why am I not noticed

I try to get your attention

But you seemed unfocused

That I'm not worth the time

For you to take a second

I know that I walk super slow

That I just can't move and go

That my body sometimes can be drag

But I thought you would be there for me

But instead you left quickly

And now I'm sitting alone

Feeling so lonely

I can't stop

But I think you don't

See or care for who I have become

You don't even text or call my phone

Why am I not noticed

I try to get your attention

But you seemed unfocused

That I'm not worth the time

For you to take a second.

Oh Hattie May

Inspiration: Honestly, this poem makes me feel a little embarrassed, because I would have to admit that felt jealous at one point. Jealousy is something that I hate admitting, because I always wanted to be known as a person who can rise above and be humble to all that God has given unto me. However, in this life, it becomes difficult not to be jealous of people who have things that you desperately want; especially, if they complain about it often. This poem is a representation of my jealousy of someone. I have felt jealous of this person, because they have a lot of things I could only dream of. But they constantly take for granted the blessings they've had in their lives. I wish I could say that I'm not jealous anymore of that person; however, I cannot. I have to admit that I am thankful for everything God has done for me. With that being said, it does hurt emotionally when I'm reminded that I cannot do something that someone else can do (especially since their a loved one).

Oh Hattie may

Excited for the new day

Blessed and favored

For your emotions are layered

Happy in a moment

Complaining that your over it

Oh Hattie May

God has given you so much

But it's never enough

No no no

Riding around in your shiny car blessed

And then say the situation is a mess

Oh Hattie may

When will you stop

Does everything just have to drop

You have money and clothes

And something for your toed

Not many people can say I know

Oh Hattie May

You whine, you dine, and you say the same lines

And the truth of the matter is

Everybody gives you dimes

So Hattie May

Please stop crying

Because I need dimes

That I can call mine

Silent No More

Inspiration: As any person in the LGBTQIA+ Community can probably testify, coming out is scary experience. There is always a chance that your loved ones may reject you, shame you, or even dismiss you out of their lives. Coming out can be traumatic for someone with an orthodox Christian family; which was my case. I've experienced a lot of religious trauma when I was shamed and rejected by multiple love ones. After coming out, it felt that I was alone; event though I wasn't physically alone. Figuring out a part of yourself, only to be told you are abominable and that you're going to hell, is self-esteem damaging. I've prayed multiple times that my loved ones would accept me and love me for who he has made me to be. Ever since my coming out, I have been prone to hide my true feelings about certain things. This poem is what I would love to say to those loved ones. This is not a disrespectful or "out of line" poem. This poem is how I felt, and I feel when those loved ones judge me for something I had no control over. This is me saying, "I will not be silent anymore".

Yes mam but

No sir I

Can I just talk

Thank you

You keep speaking

But none of you are listening

You are too busy fighting correctness

But who is fighting for my best interest

I only have one life

This is my time

Instead of being supportive

You've been self-assertive

I tried to speak my mind

But it's never the right time

How can yall do this?

When I didn't choose it?

This is me

Extra, gay, and sweet

I won't lie

Because we're all running out of time

I like boys and that's my truth

But will that ever sooth you

Are you upset because I'm gay

Then ask God why he made me this way

I can't be silent any longer

But it is I, who has to say I'm stronger

I'm stronger than hate

I've overcame my own weight

I'm stronger than rejection

I've always had the best intentions

I'm stronger than what people have assumed

Because I've beaten obstacles, that they would have all lose

New Self

Inspiration: Recently, I started gaining some attractions for females. My attraction to males is still present and active, but now I think of girls as sexually attractive people to. At this point in my life, I'm not sure if its my maturity in age or am I seriously attracted to females. I wrote this poem to help me cope with how I feel because I haven't told anyone except one family member and a friend. I'm nervous publishing this poem, but I want someone to know that it's okay to know yourself at one moment and not the next. I don't know where my sexuality will lead. All I know is that I figuring out more about myself day by day, and I feel that everyone is too.

I'm 23

I'm somewhere I never thought I would be

I can't believe I'm still learning

Its hard to believe that I'm growing

I though I knew myself in and out

But life keeps turning around

I always seen myself as one way

But God may have more to say

Since I young I knew I like guys

But now I think I may be Bi

I'm emotionally stuck

While figure out, like what the F**K

I never been attracted to girls, so why now

And just listen to how crazy this sounds

I'm scared to say anything

Because this will change everything

What will my family say

Will they believe that I'm no longer gay

I don't know what I am

But I going to find out with the help with some fam

Resources

Purple Rain: The Stories of My Tears is a poem book that is supposed to help someone to cope and provide emotional support to anyone in need. With that being, I want to make sure that anyone who is in need is aware of multiple resources they can use to help them in their lives.

Though I am not able to stat, in this book, exactly what resources you can use, please feel free to email me if you are in need of any resources and would like my help to connect you with an organization. My email can be found on my bio (on the next page).

If you are currently experiencing any thoughts of harming yourself or other, please call 911 or the national suicide hotline (988). This hotline is anonymous and free to everyone. Please take care of yourself and please know that you are loved. Even if you feel that you are not loved, you are loved by me. Peace and Love to you all.

Author's Bio

Name: Johnathan Jones

Pronouns: He/ Him/ His

Hometown: Kingsland, Ga

Religion: Christian

Favorite Color: Purple

Favorite Hobby: Cooking and Writing

Sexuality: Gay (Currently Bi-Curious)

Education: Bachelors of Social Work from Fort Valley State University and Currently pursuing a Master's of Social Work at the University of Georgia.

Occupation: Full-Time Graduate Student/Social Worker

Email: socialwork.jones@gmail.com

What made you start writing?: I started writing as a coping mechanism to help cope with everything life gave me. I was able to identify in 4 different oppressed communities by the age of 13. I had to start writing because it was the only way I felt my voice being heard. Writing was how I could feel my feelings, scream in words, and I could control what I wanted the reader to know. Writing was my partial escape.

Why expose yourself publicly, when you mention a lot of personal emotions?: I wrote this book because I wanted others to know that they are not alone. I felt alone most of my life. I felt that no one could understand me and that I have to accept that I just got a crappy hand I life. However, as I got older, I realize that I can't have that mentality. I wanted others, who may feel invisible, to know that they are not alone.

Made in the USA
Columbia, SC
03 December 2022